SCIENTIFIC AMERICAN | EDUCATIONAL PUBLISHING

SCIENTIFIC AMERICAN INVESTIGATES CAREERS IN SCIENCE

METEOROLOGIST

BY ROSIE BANKS

Published in 2025 by The Rosen Publishing Group
in association with Scientific American Educational Publishing
2544 Clinton Street, Buffalo NY 14224

Library of Congress Cataloging-in-Publication Data
Names: Banks, Rosie, 1978-.
Title: Meteorologist / Rosie Banks.
Description: New York : Scientific American Educational Publishing, an imprint of Rosen Publishing, 2025. | Series: Scientific American investigates careers in science | Includes glossary and index.
Identifiers: ISBN 9781725352377 (pbk.) | ISBN 9781725352384 (library bound) | ISBN 9781725352391 (ebook)
Subjects: LCSH: Meteorology–Vocational guidance–Juvenile literature. | Meteorologists–Juvenile literature.
Classification: LCC QC869.5 B36 2025 | DDC 551.5023–dc23

Designer: Leslie Taylor
Editor: Therese Shea

Portions of this work were originally authored by Kristen Rajczak and published as *Be an Meteorologist*. All new material in this edition is authored by Rosie Banks.

Photo credits: Cover (main) Frame Stock Footage/Shutterstock.com; series art (background) jijomathaidesigners/Shutterstock.com; p. 5 izusek/iStockphoto.com, (inset) little_nm/Shutterstock.com; p. 7 (Aristotle) Ludovisi Collection/File:Aristotle Altemps Inv8575.jpg_commons.wikimedia.org, (inset book) Biblioteca Europea di Informazione e Cultura/File:Tomus sextus operum Aristotelis Stagiritae V00235 00000004.tif_commons.wikimedia.org, (inset planes) Ivan Cholakov/Shutterstock.com; p. 9 Gorodenkoff/Shutterstock.com; p. 11 Jevtic/iStockphoto.com; p. 13 Milkovasa/Shutterstock.com; p. p. 15 milehightraveler/iStockphoto.com; p. 17 Dennis MacDonald/Shutterstock.com; p. 18 Vasyl Shulga/Shutterstock.com; p. 19 JENNIFER E. WOLF/iStockphoto.com; p. 21 Toa55/iStockphoto.com; p. 23 (top) Alex Erwin/Shutterstock.com, (bottom) EPH610/Shutterstock.com; p. 25 aappp/Shutterstock.com; p. 26 Dennis MacDonald/Shutterstock.com; p. 27 BrookePierce/iStockphoto.com; p. 28 Aree_S/Shutterstock.com.

Some of the images in this book illustrate individuals who are models. The depictions do not imply actual situations or events.

Printed in the United States of America

CPSIA compliance information: Batch #CWSA25. For Further Information contact Rosen Publishing at 1-800-237-9932.

CONTENTS

Words in the glossary appear in **bold** type the first time they are used in the text.

CAREER ABOUT THE ATMOSPHERE

Did you ever lie on your back and watch the clouds go by? This is a great way to observe how Earth's atmosphere is always changing. The state of the atmosphere at any time and place is called the weather. Some kinds of weather we can see, such as rain and snow. Some we can't see, such as the amount of humidity, or water vapor, in the air.

There are scientists who monitor, or watch, what's going on in Earth's atmosphere. They use many kinds of tools. They can tell us what atmospheric measurements mean for our weather and try to forecast the weather in the future too.

FUN FACT

WEATHER IS AN EVENT OR EVENTS—SUCH AS A STORM OR COLD DAY—THAT HAPPENS OVER HOURS, DAYS, OR WEEKS. CLIMATE IS THE AVERAGE WEATHER IN A PLACE OVER 30 YEARS OR MORE.

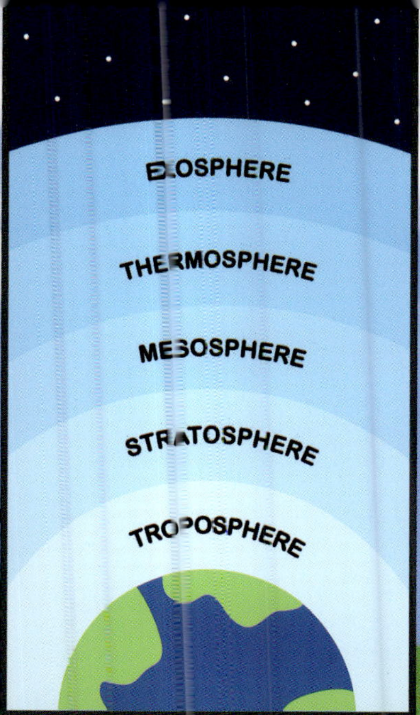

The atmosphere is the mix of gases around Earth. It's made up of layers. The lowest layer, the troposphere, is where most weather happens.

Meteorology Matters

Forecasting, or predicting the weather using facts, is just one part of a meteorologist's job. Meteorologists are scientists who study Earth's atmosphere. The science of meteorology examines the causes of and changes in weather and climate. Meteorologists are also concerned with how people's activities affect Earth's atmosphere.

WEATHER HISTORY

For thousands of years, people have studied and recorded the weather. By the mid-1400s, a tool had been invented to measure humidity. The thermometer was invented around 1610 and the barometer, which measures **atmospheric pressure**, was invented around 1643.

By the 1800s, even more meteorological tools had been introduced to help scientists make sense of the weather around them. They began to understand that weather moves in systems across Earth, which allowed for limited forecasting. When the **telegraph** was introduced, helping people to communicate over long distances, weather observations and reports could be shared more easily.

FUN FACT

THE SUCCESS OF WORLD WAR II (1939–1945) MILITARY OPERATIONS DEPENDED ON WEATHER. NEW **TECHNOLOGY** FOR METEOROLOGY HAPPENED BECAUSE THE MILITARY NEEDED BETTER FORECASTS.

Aristotle of ancient Greece wrote a book called *Meteorologica* around 340 BCE, which included weather observations. ("Meteorology" comes from a Greek word meaning "something that happens high in the sky.")

GETTING STARTED

If you're interested in the weather and how to forecast it, you should think about becoming a meteorologist. The first step to becoming a meteorologist is doing well in school. In high school, you should take all the math and science classes you can, especially **physics**, earth science, and a math class called calculus. These subjects will help you once you begin studying meteorology in college—and a college **degree** is a requirement for meteorologists.

Meteorologists also work with computers, computer programs, and other science tools. Being comfortable with and knowledgeable about technology is key to succeeding in this science.

Not every weather presenter on TV is a meteorologist. Some just report the weather reports they receive from meteorologists.

Supercomputers

Meteorologists use some of the fastest and most powerful computers in the world. Different weather conditions are entered into weather computer programs that can create models of weather systems. The models present how weather might happen in real life. This allows meteorologists to see what might occur days or weeks into the future.

COLLEGE DAYS

Not all colleges have degrees in meteorology, but many have similar degrees, such as atmospheric science. Computer science, math, and physics are also helpful degrees for those who may wish to go on to earn a higher degree, such as a master's degree in meteorology. A higher degree may open the door to more jobs too.

Before becoming a meteorologist, many students follow a working meteorologist around for a time. Students often complete an **internship** at a weather station or atmospheric **research** center. Watching a real scientist do their job can help young people understand more about the daily duties of this career.

FUN FACT

METEOROLOGISTS WHO WORK FOR THE U.S. NATIONAL WEATHER SERVICE MUST HAVE A COLLEGE DEGREE IN METEOROLOGY, ATMOSPHERIC SCIENCE, OR ANOTHER NATURAL SCIENCE FIELD THAT INCLUDES CLASSES IN THESE SUBJECTS.

Meteorologists who want to do scientific research commonly must have a higher degree. In school, they'll specialize, or focus, on a kind of meteorology, such as agricultural meteorology, which has to do with weather's effects on farming.

NARROWING THE FIELD

So, you've decided to become a meteorologist. Great! But what kind? The meteorologist you're probably most familiar with is called a broadcast meteorologist. They work at TV and radio stations explaining the weather forecast for others to understand. People depend on broadcast meteorologists' reports to plan their outdoor activities. Broadcast meteorologists are also the ones who warn the public about extreme weather, such as snowstorms and **hurricanes**.

Some meteorologists go to school for an engineering degree. This would be a helpful area of study for someone hoping to become an instrument specialist. These scientists design new tools and methods for recording the weather.

Knowing how to use meteorological instruments is important for all meteorologists, such as those who might work at this airport weather station.

FUN FACT

WEATHER FORECASTERS ARE METEOROLOGISTS WHO USE COMPUTERS AND COMPUTER MODELS, OR PROGRAMS, TO MAKE WEATHER REPORTS AND FORECASTS.

Research meteorologists are the scientists trying to find out something new about the atmosphere. They may focus on one topic, such as lightning or hurricanes. They spend their time gathering measurements and other data, or facts and numbers, and figuring out what they mean.

One type of research meteorologist is a climatologist. Climatologists study climate using weather records from past years. They look for changes over time and predict future climate conditions. Archive meteorologists also look at past weather records to make sure they're accurate, or exact and free of mistakes. Different kinds of meteorologists work together. Sharing knowledge saves time—and sometimes even lives when dangerous weather is on its way.

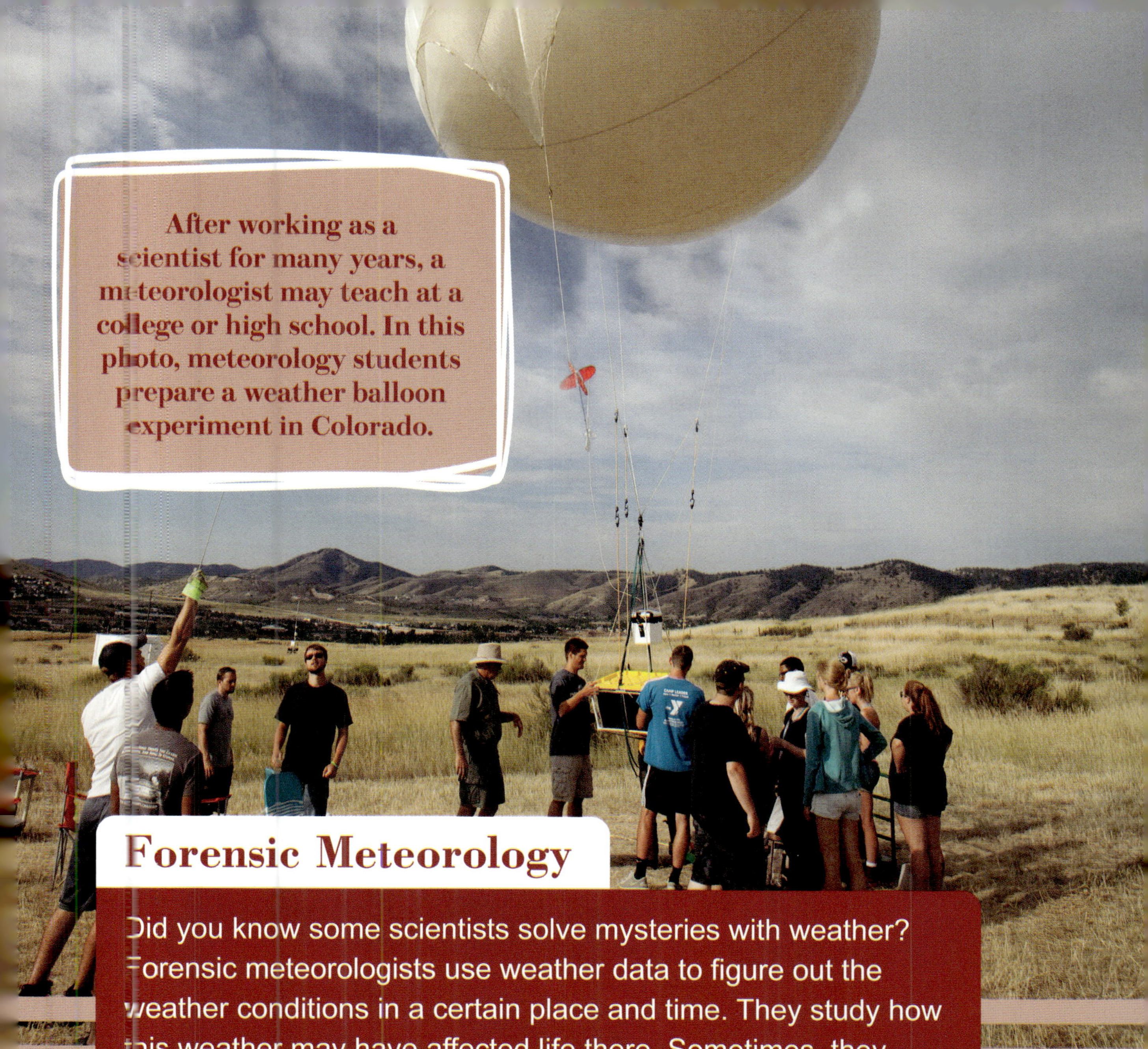

After working as a scientist for many years, a meteorologist may teach at a college or high school. In this photo, meteorology students prepare a weather balloon experiment in Colorado.

Forensic Meteorology

Did you know some scientists solve mysteries with weather? Forensic meteorologists use weather data to figure out the weather conditions in a certain place and time. They study how this weather may have affected life there. Sometimes, they must figure out if weather could have caused accidents, fires, or other events.

HELP WANTED

Imagine you now have a degree and are a meteorologist. You need a job next! The U.S. government is the largest employer of meteorologists in the nation. Many work for the National Oceanic and Atmospheric Administration (NOAA) or the National Aeronautics and Space Administration (NASA).

Meteorologists are also a key part of the U.S. military. Knowing weather conditions and how they might change is a central piece of planning some kinds of military operations. Air force and navy missions, for example, need to avoid dangerous weather conditions in the air and on water. Meteorologists are stationed at U.S. military bases around the world.

FUN FACT

THE NATIONAL WEATHER SERVICE'S MISSION IS TO "PROVIDE WEATHER, WATER, AND CLIMATE DATA, FORECASTS AND WARNINGS FOR THE PROTECTION OF LIFE AND PROPERTY AND ENHANCEMENT [IMPROVEMENT] OF THE NATIONAL ECONOMY."

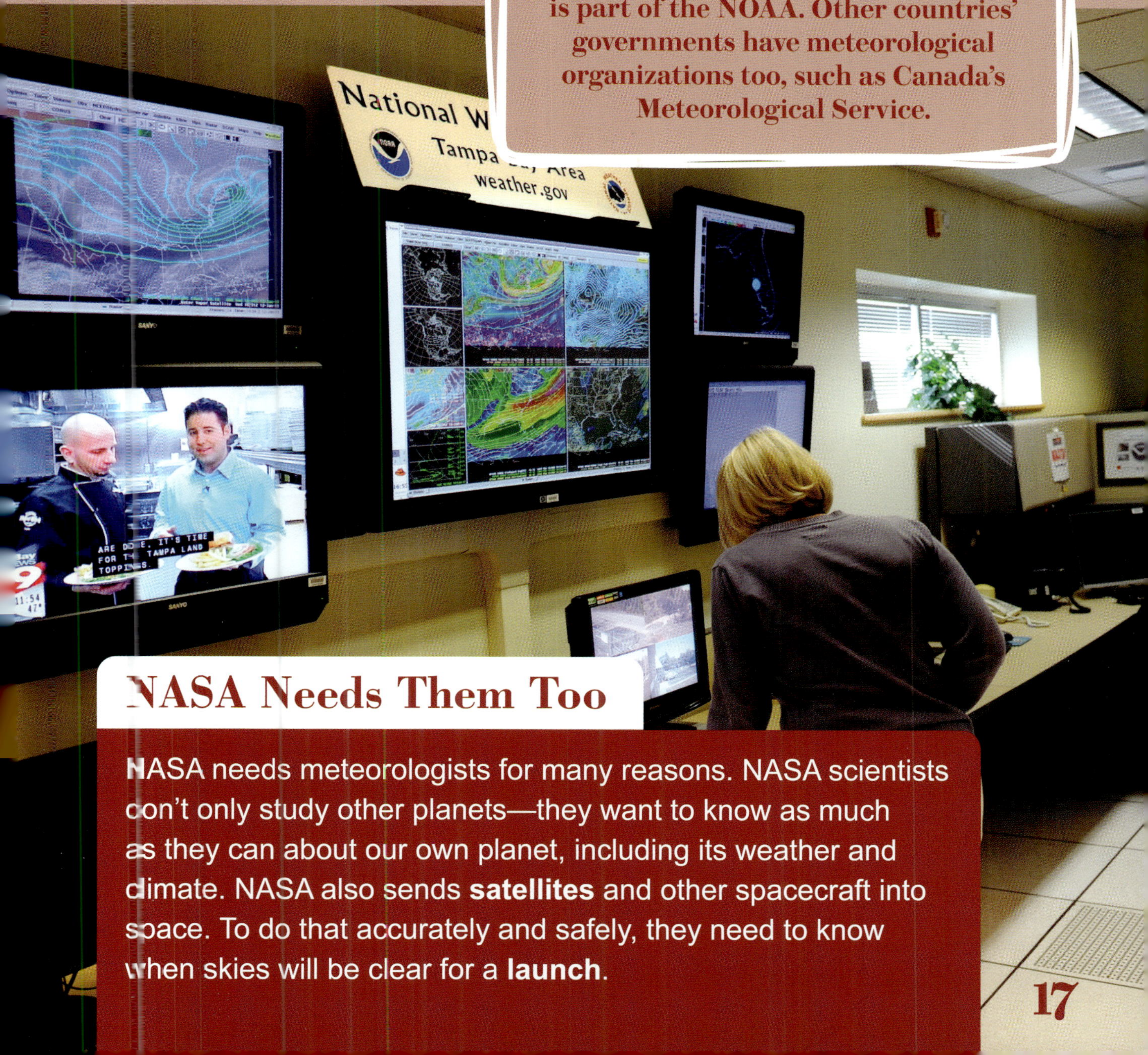

The National Weather Service (NWS) is part of the NOAA. Other countries' governments have meteorological organizations too, such as Canada's Meteorological Service.

NASA Needs Them Too

NASA needs meteorologists for many reasons. NASA scientists don't only study other planets—they want to know as much as they can about our own planet, including its weather and climate. NASA also sends **satellites** and other spacecraft into space. To do that accurately and safely, they need to know when skies will be clear for a **launch**.

Beyond the government, certain businesses need knowledge of weather and climate. For example, property **insurance** companies might hire meteorologists. An understanding of weather conditions helps them know what risks people's homes and other property face from floods and storms. Transportation businesses, including airlines, need to know how weather may affect travel.

Energy companies that depend on wind or solar power plan their operations according to the climate of different locations. Boating and fishing businesses also need to know when it's too dangerous to go out. Some of these companies hire their own meteorologists. Others buy information from private forecasting companies that employ meteorologists.

Construction companies need to know if places are likely to flood or experience any other kind of storm damage.

Football and Forecasts

National Football League (NFL) teams have hired meteorologists too! The weather has a big impact on the game. Rain makes everything slippery, so players need to know how to handle and pass the ball in different conditions. A football can deflate, or lose air pressure, in cold weather. Winds can affect the accuracy of kicking as well.

WHERE THEY WORK

Meteorologists need data to do their work. Many work in weather centers. There, they collect data from instruments on the ground and from satellites around Earth. Other times, they need to travel to distant weather stations.

NWS Weather Forecast Offices have meteorologists on duty 24 hours a day every day of the year. Short-term forecasters there work on the weather for the next one to two days. Long-term forecasters are also on duty using the latest data to improve forecasts further into the future. Some meteorologists go to places during **emergency** events, such as blizzards and wildfires. They inform the public of what's going on and how to stay safe.

Meteorologists can help people who fight wildfires figure out which way winds will blow so the firefighters can be prepared to stop the spread.

Watch or Warning?

Meteorologists are the first line of defense against severe weather. The National Weather Service issues a "watch" if the conditions are right for bad weather to happen, such as **tornadoes** or flooding. The NWS issues a "warning" when a weather event is actually happening. Conditions can change, so not every watch turns into a warning.

TECHNOLOGY OF METEOROLOGY

Meteorologists need many kinds of data to get an accurate idea of the weather and how it might change. So, they use many different tools, also called instruments. Radar, which stands for radio detection and ranging, finds and measures precipitation using radio waves. Doppler radar is a special kind of radar used to measure precipitation as well as wind speed and direction.

Satellites allow meteorologists to see weather systems moving around the planet. Early weather satellites could only show pictures, but today, satellites also monitor wind speed, temperature, and other atmospheric conditions. NASA launched four NOAA satellites between 2016 and 2024.

FUN FACT

DID YOU EVER WONDER WHAT A WEATHER BALLOON DOES? IT CARRIES A WEATHER INSTRUMENT CALLED A RADIOSONDE, WHICH CAN MEASURE AIR PRESSURE, WIND SPEED, TEMPERATURE, AND HUMIDITY IN THE UPPER TROPOSPHERE AND EVEN THE LOWER STRATOSPHERE.

Specially equipped aircraft can fly right into weather systems, providing real-time data. This is the P-3 NOAA Hurricane Hunter aircraft.

More Meteorological Instruments

INSTRUMENT	WHAT IT MEASURES
thermometer	temperature
hygrometer	humidity
barometer	air pressure
rain gauge	amount of rainfall
anenometer	wind speed and direction
disdrometer	size and velocity (speed and direction) of raindrops

Many people have weather instruments such as thermometers and rain gauges at home.

FIGURING OUT THE FORECAST

The forecast takes a lot of data and a lot of teamwork between different scientists. Meteorologists first collect data from satellites, radiosondes, radar, and other instruments from weather stations at the surface and in the air. They use this data to get an accurate picture of the state of the atmosphere at that moment. This doesn't happen just once a day. Rather, data is collected several times a day by thousands of weather stations on land and at sea.

Data is shared among world weather centers located in Russia, the United States, the United Kingdom, and Australia. This helps scientists around the world get a better picture of global weather patterns.

FUN FACT

WEATHER FORECAST ACCURACY HAS IMPROVED A LOT. METEOROLOGISTS' FIVE-DAY FORECASTS TODAY ARE BETTER THAN 24-HOUR FORECASTS IN 1980!

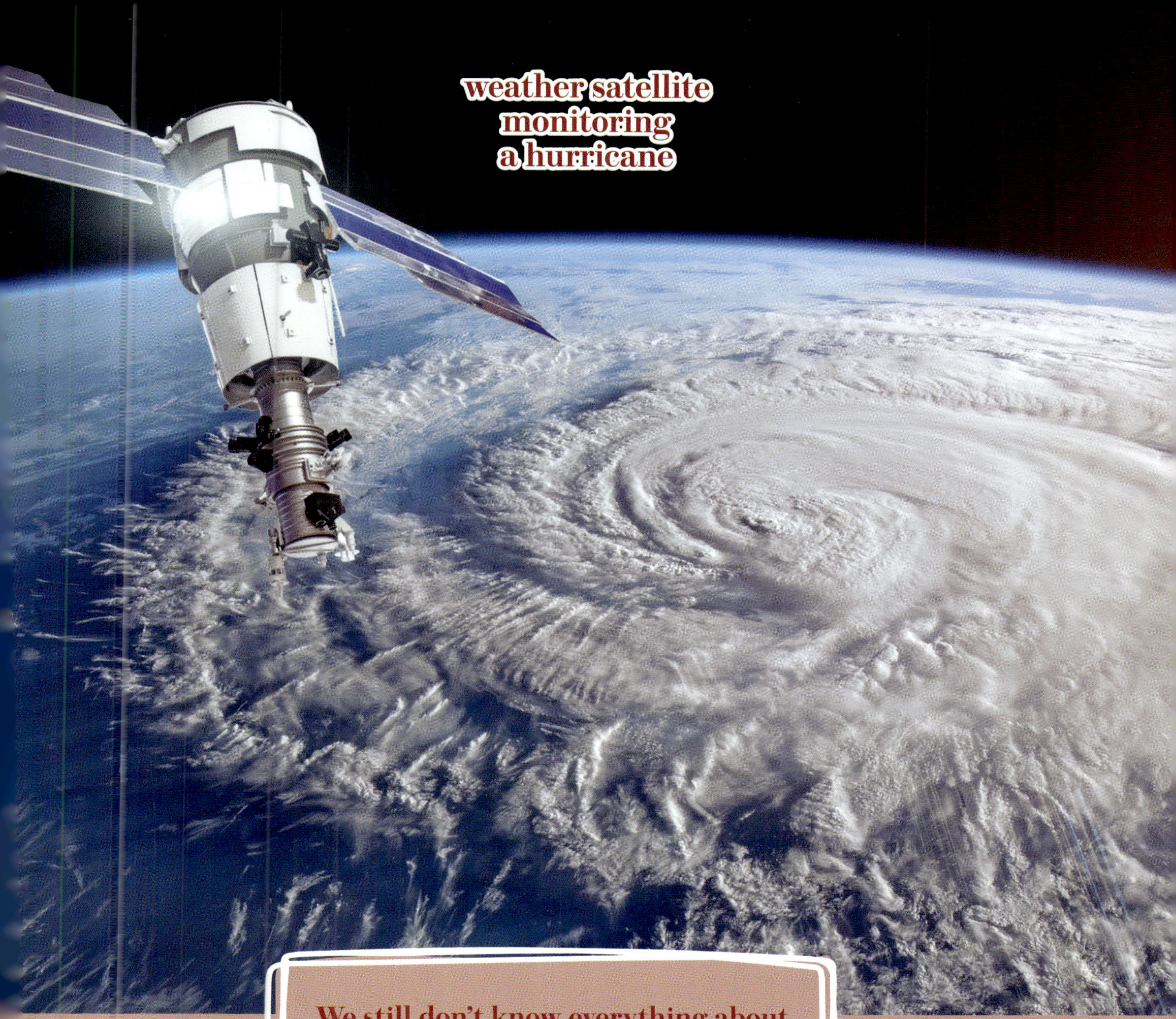
weather satellite monitoring a hurricane

We still don't know everything about why conditions change in Earth's atmosphere. That makes forecasting challenging at times.

The data collected by world weather centers, including the National Weather Service in Washington, DC, is then sent to NWS offices all over the United States. From there, local meteorologists use the data and their understanding of local conditions to make forecasts in their area. Computer models help with the forecasts. Broadcast meteorologists or weather reporters then share these forecasts with the public.

Just one weather station wouldn't be able to collect enough data to make any weather predictions. A forecast is only possible because of the work of thousands of meteorologists around the world.

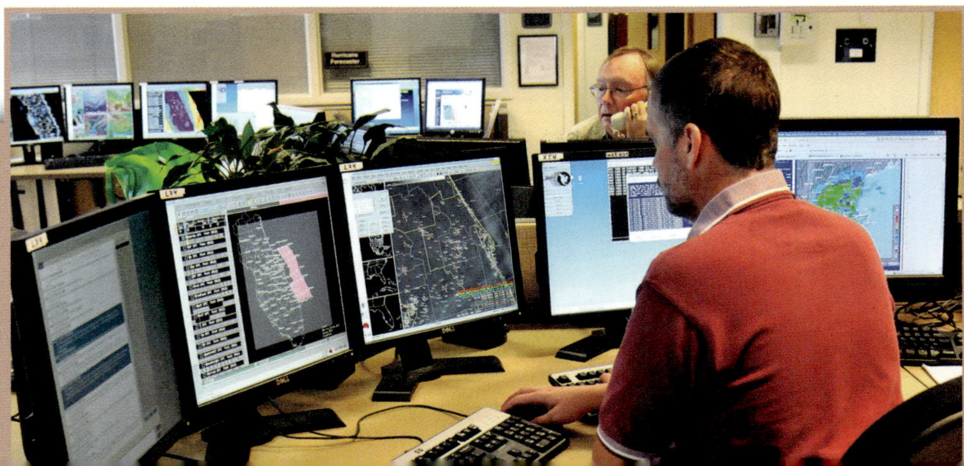

Forecasts make our lives easier in many ways, but they can also save lives.

Not Just Forecasts

Meteorologists are some of the scientists working to learn more about the effects of global **climate change**, including the slow warming of the atmosphere and oceans. Meteorologists are studying the problems climate change may cause, such as an increase in destructive storms. They're working on solutions to these problems too.

MAKING A DIFFERENCE

As new weather technology is designed, meteorologists can forecast with even more accuracy. This is so important for severe weather events, including hurricanes and tornadoes. The more accurate the forecast before a weather event, the more time people have to prepare for it. Sometimes people must leave their homes, which may be in danger due to weather conditions.

Many scientists think our warming planet will bring more severe weather events. It may even make these events harder to forecast. This will bring another challenge for future meteorologists. They will be needed more than ever to keep people safe and informed about the weather.

What Kind of Meteorology Career?

Careers in Meteorology

FORECASTING
predict weather conditions and issue watches and warnings when needed

RESEARCH
study a weather topic or develop new tools and methods

TEACHING
help others understand the science of meteorology and its importance

MILITARY
report weather and forecasts for military operations

GOVERNMENT
work in research, forecasting, or emergency situations

PRIVATE COMPANIES
help businesses, such as airlines, energy companies, farms, and construction

FORENSIC
research the weather of the past

BROADCASTING
report weather conditions and forecast to audiences

Weather matters in so many areas of life, so meteorologists have a number of career choices.

GLOSSARY

atmospheric pressure: A downward force caused by the weight of the atmosphere.

climate change: Long-term change in Earth's climate, caused partly by human activities such as burning oil and natural gas.

degree: An official paper given to someone who has completed certain classes at a college or university.

emergency: An unexpected situation that needs quick action.

hurricane: A powerful storm that forms over water and causes heavy rainfall and high winds.

insurance: An agreement in which a person pays a company for a guarantee of money in case of damage, illness, or death.

internship: A supervised job experience, usually completed by a student.

launch: The sending out of something, such as a rocket, with great force.

physics: The study of matter, energy, force, and motion, and the relationships among them.

research: Studying to find something new.

satellite: An object that circles Earth to collect and send information or aid in communication.

technology: Using science, engineering, and other industries to invent useful tools or to solve problems. Also, a machine, piece of equipment, or method created by technology.

telegraph: A method of communicating using electric signals sent through wires.

tornado: A funnel-shaped cloud of fast winds that often causes destruction.

FOR MORE INFORMATION

Books

Harasymiw, Martin. *Meteorology*. New York, NY: Gareth Stevens Publishing, 2025.

Olson, Elsie. *Meteorology Lab: Explore Weather with Art & Activities*. Minneapolis, MN: Abdo, 2024.

Peterson, Megan Cooley. *Understanding Weather*. North Mankato, MN: Pebble, 2021.

Websites

Careers in Meteorology
www.noaa.gov/careers/meteorology
Read more about this science as well as about real-life meteorologists.

National Weather Service
www.weather.gov
Explore weather maps, forecasts, satellite images, and more on the NWS website.

Resources for Students
www.weather.gov/cae/justforkids.html
The NWS has a page with links for young people interested in a career in weather.

Publisher's note to educators and parents: Our editors have carefully reviewed these websites to ensure that they are suitable for students. Many websites change frequently, however, and we cannot guarantee that a site's future contents will continue to meet our high standards of quality and educational value. Be advised that students should be closely supervised whenever they access the internet.

INDEX